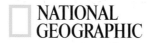

Living Things Need Water

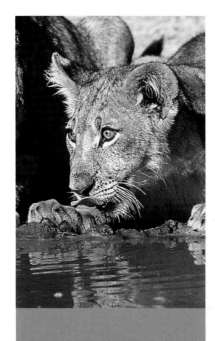

Sharon Street

Birds need water.

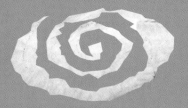

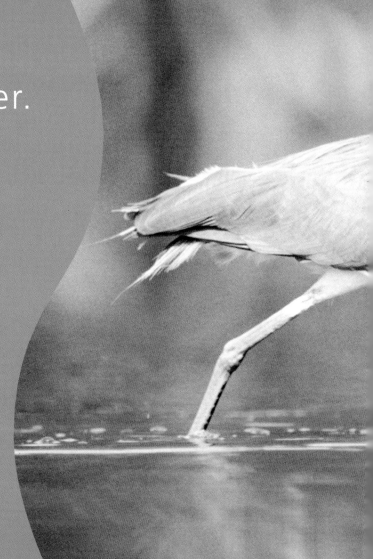

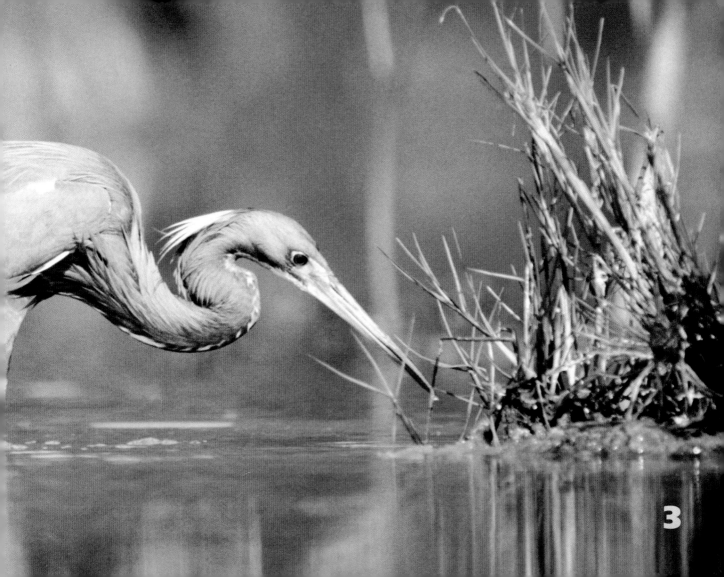

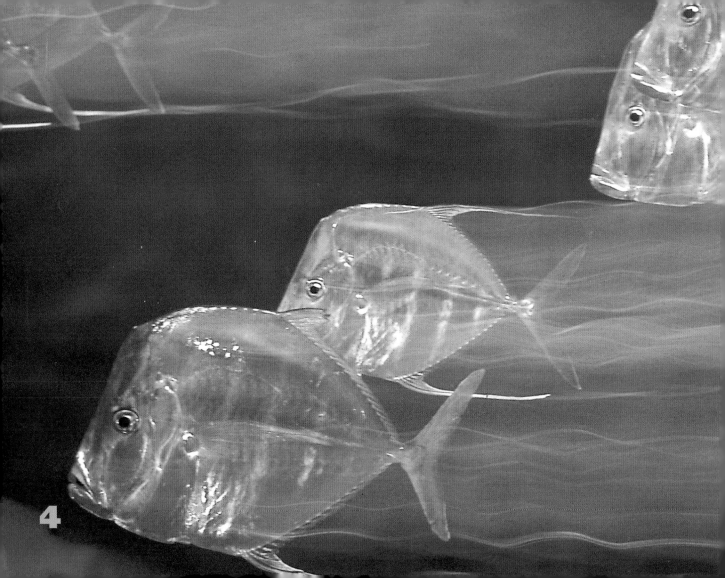

4

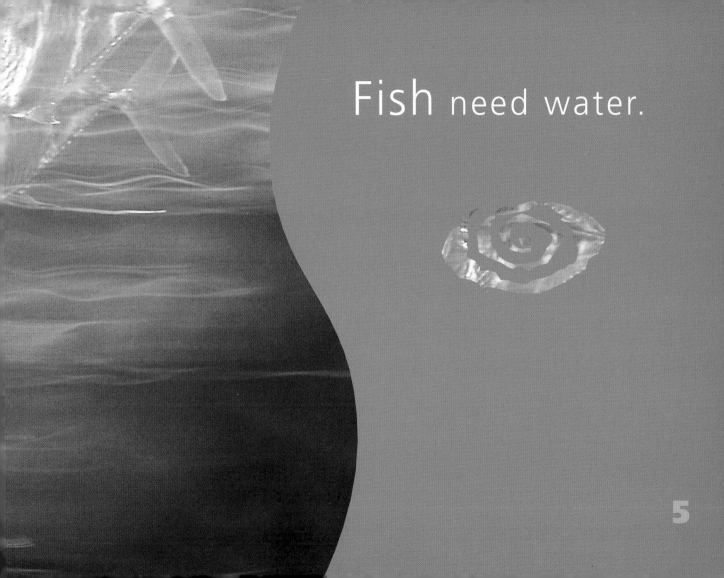

Fish need water.

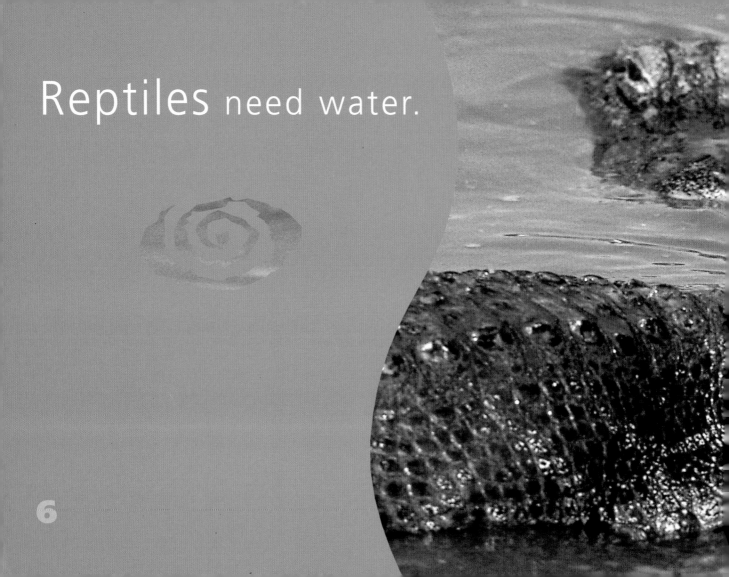

Reptiles need water.

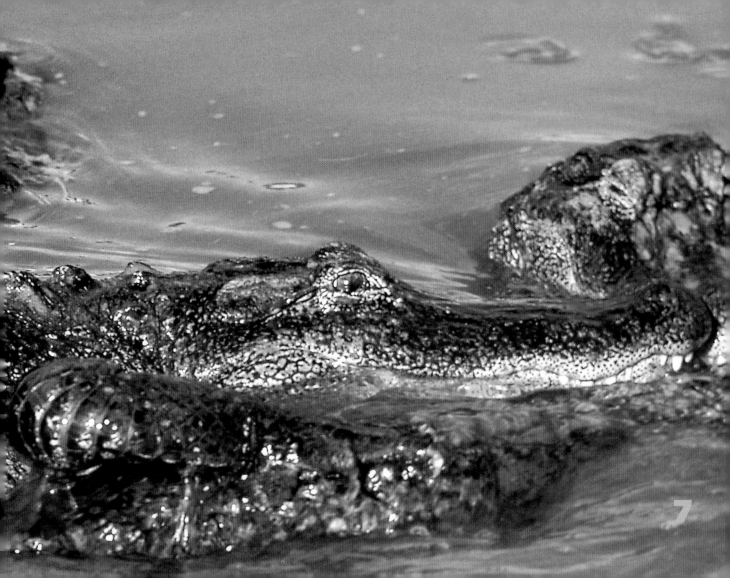

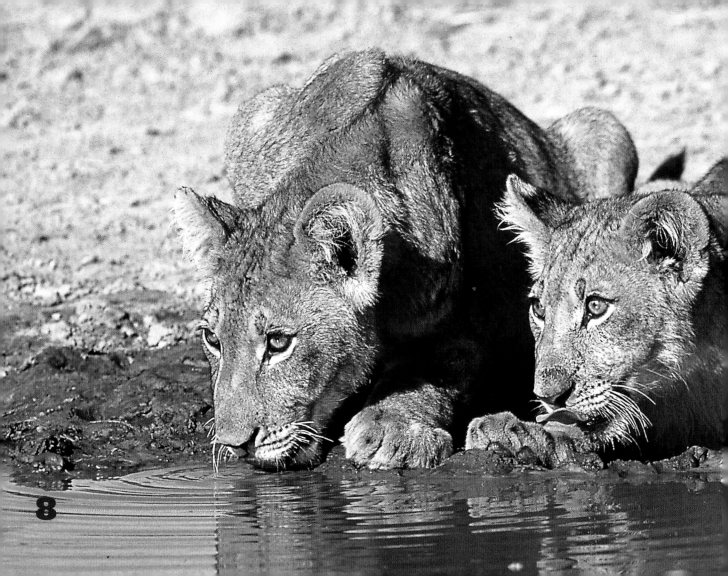

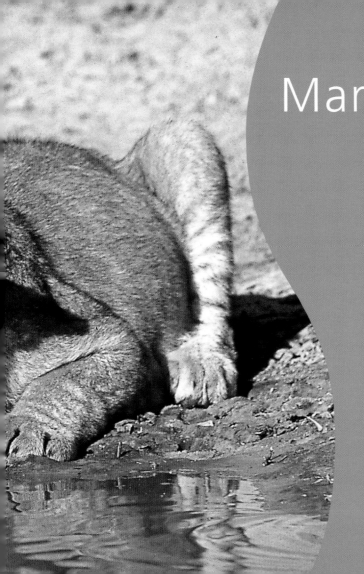

Mammals need water.

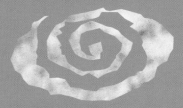

9

Plants need water.

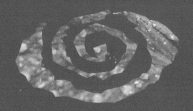

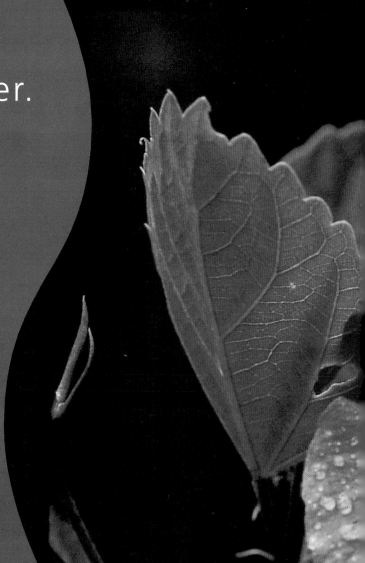

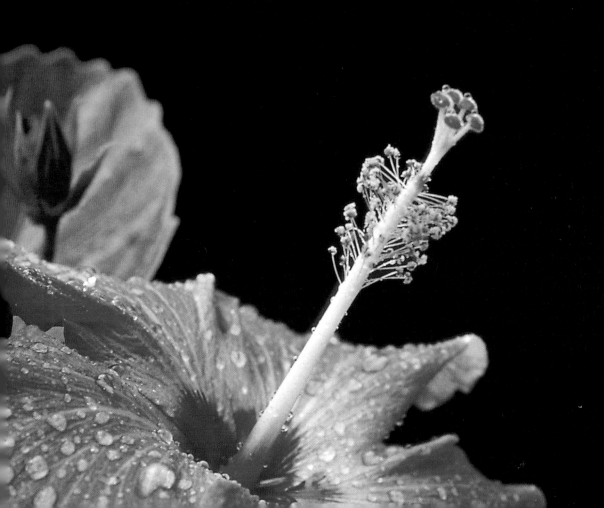

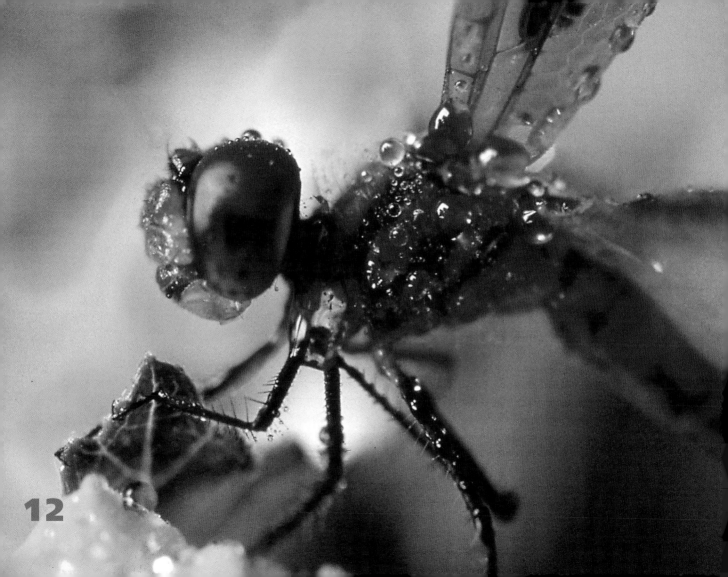

12

Insects need water.

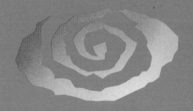

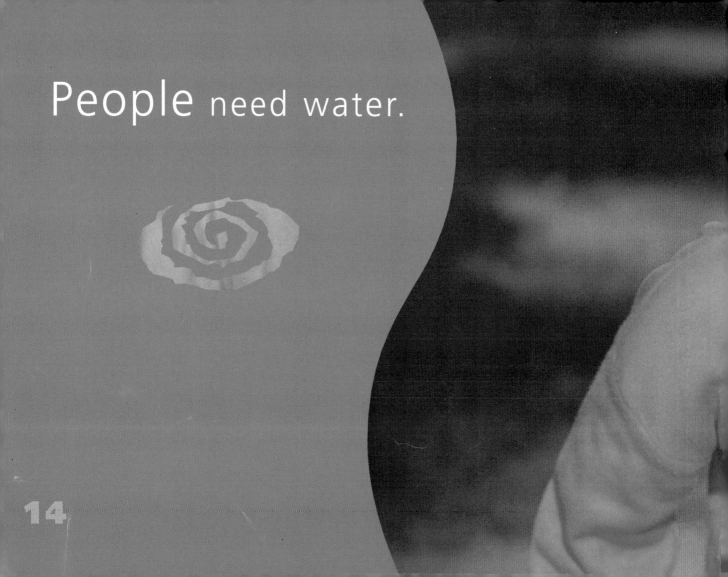

People need water.

14

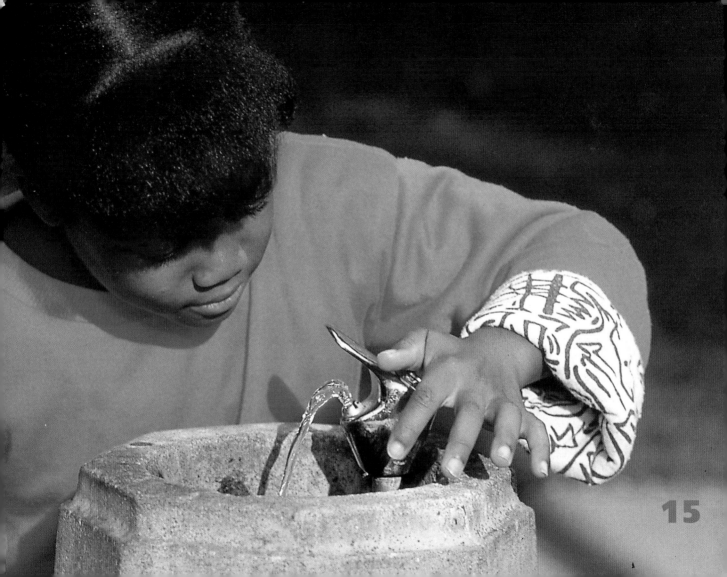

15

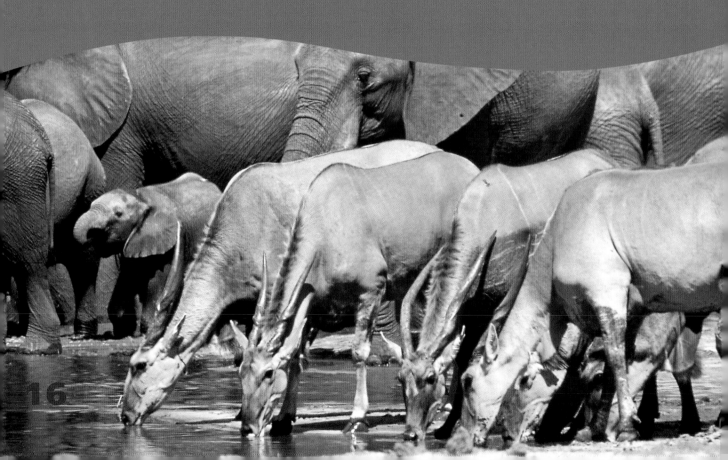

All living things need water.